7/94

A QUARTO BOOK

Library of Congress Catalog Card Number: 93-087763

ISBN 0-376-02759-2

This book was designed and produced by
Quarto Publishing Inc.
The Old Brewery, 6 Blundell Street
London N7 9BH

Editors: Kate Kirby, Laura Washburn, Susan Ward
Art Editor: Mark Stevens
Designer: Julie Francis
Art Director: Moira Clinch
Editorial Director: Sophie Collins

Illustrations © Alison Barratt

First published in North America in 1994 by Sunset Publishing Corporation
Menlo Park, CA 94025

First printing May 1994

Typeset in Great Britain by West End Studios, Eastbourne, UK
Manufactured in Singapore by Eray Scan Pte. Ltd.
Printed in China by Leefung-Asco Printers Ltd.

— THE GOURMET KITCHEN —
VINEGARS

WRITTEN BY GINA STEER
ILLUSTRATED BY ALISON BARRATT

SUNSET PUBLISHING CORPORATION
MENLO PARK, CALIFORNIA

Contents

INTRODUCTION

*N*o kitchen is complete without a good selection of vinegars, whether they be basic vinegars, flavored "boutique" vinegars, or a combination of the two. Vinegars offer a surprisingly wide range of uses: as a medium for pickling and preserving; as a flavor enhancer alone or in combination with other ingredients; as a tenderizer in marinades; as an aromatic condiment, such as basil vinegar drizzled over tomato salad.

There was a time when the only vinegar sold in the supermarket was made from distilled cider. Thankfully, life has progressed considerably, as have the varieties of vinegar now available to the gourmet cook. Today, along with the usual wine

vinegars — white, red, champagne, and tarragon-flavored — and cider vinegars, there is a veritable host of flavors to choose from. Their very names conjure up a wealth of gastronomic delights that positively tingle the taste buds — orange, black currant, balsamic, garlic, and peppercorn to name just a few.

As a rule, the choice of vinegar for any dish depends on the ethnic origins of the recipe. But one of the great beauties of cooking is its versatility. So try experimenting. Chefs do it, so why not you?

Other Uses of Vinegar

In addition to being an important ingredient in cooking, vinegar has other household uses. It can be used as an antiseptic for minor cuts and abrasions; for reducing the effect of insect bites and stings; or as an effective mouthwash and gargle, especially when combined with honey. (The latter is also particularly helpful for sore throats.) Try adding vinegar to bath water to help relieve aching, tired muscles, or to rinse water to achieve beautiful shining hair.

5

What is Vinegar?

Vinegar comes from the French *vin aigre,* meaning sour wine, but vinegar is also made from barley. Its development, a natural process, occurs when alcohol has been converted by acid-forming bacteria (much the same as milk is soured by lactic bacteria). The flavors found in the original wine or barley will impart either fruity or aromatic flavors to the vinegar.

Originally vinegar was made by leaving ale or wine standing in the open, where it "turned" and became vinegar. Nowadays it is commercially brewed. First, starch in wine or barley is converted to sugar; then, added yeast turns the sugar to alcohol. Next, naturally occuring acetic acid bacterium (a vinegar "mother") is added, encouraging bacteria to grow and turning the alcohol into vinegar. Finally, the vinegar is pumped into large vats where it is left to mature until ready for bottling.

Basic Vinegars

Wine vinegars are made from all types of wine from many different regions of the world. Though it may sound obvious, the better the wine, the better the vinegar. Even a particular type of wine vinegar can be made in a variety of ways. For example, sherry vinegar is made from sherry; it can be produced within a year or over a period of years, and it might be decanted into progressively smaller barrels in order to mature and deepen the flavor, as with a fine cognac.

Balsamic vinegar, considered by many to be the ultimate vinegar, has been made in Modena, Italy, since the 16th century. In those early days, it was a valuable commodity and was often included in a bride's dowry or as a prized legacy in a will. Dark, rich, sweet, and pungent, balsamic is made from the fermented juice of Trebbiano grapes. Its superb unique flavor is the result of the length and refinement of

its aging process. As with old cognac, the wooden vats which store the vinegar are of paramount importance. The woods used in the construction of the vats range from oak to walnut to cherry, each imparting its distinctive taste. Traditionally, it takes ten years for the vinegar to mature.

The type of vinegar popular in a particular country — or even a particular region — depends upon local raw materials and drinking habits. Hence wine vinegar comes from the wine-producing areas, while English malt vinegar uses the malted barley commonly used to make beer. Cider vinegar, with its more acidic flavor, is produced from cider or fermented apple juice, and typical of fruit-growing areas.

Chinese and Japanese rice vinegars vary in color, from pale to golden to almost clear. Milder than Western vinegars, Japanese vinegar is slightly sweeter. Chinese black vinegar can be made from wheat, millet, or sorghum; and like the European balsamic version, the best is matured for several years. It should have a pleasantly bitter taste and a distinctive smoky flavor.

8

Flavored Vinegars

The selection of flavored vinegars that grace supermarket and deli shelves today outstrips the imagination. Garlic, mixed herb and peppercorn, black currant, and raspberry are only four.

What could be better than a tomato and mozzarella salad drizzled with dressing made from basil-flavored vinegar or a homemade lentil soup perked up with a dash of dill vinegar? Rosemary vinegar can serve as a fragrant dressing for chicken salad or can be used to deglaze the pan after roasting a chicken. It is possible to make your own flavored vinegars, but the result will not be as strong as those commercially made. In those, the flavoring herbs, spices or fruits are steeped in the vinegar for an extended time — longer than two years.

A walk through your own garden or a trip to the local produce market can yield a rich harvest of new flavors. Pick a generous bunch of lavender flower spikes or scented roses; shake gently to dislodge any insects; rinse and air dry; then, trim the stems. Pack the flowers or petals into sterilized jars, cover with white wine vinegar, seal and leave in the dark for at least 1 month. Before serving, strain through cheesecloth.

You can also use violet petals to give subtle flavor, while nasturtium seeds impart a strong caper-like taste. Try steeping vanilla pods, shavings of coconut or horseradish, strips of citrus fruit zest, and even peanuts. The choice is yours.

Making Your Own Vinegar

To make your own vinegar, you must first make a vinegar "mother." Place two tablespoons of vinegar and half a bottle of wine or cider in a bowl; then leave in a sunny place — a window sill will do nicely — for two weeks. The skin that forms (the *aceto* bacteria) is the vinegar "mother," which is the starter that is needed to turn wine (or other alcohols) into vinegar.

10

Skim off the "mother" and transfer it — with more of the same type of alcohol — to a wide-mouthed container or bowl. Cover the opening with cheesecloth ensuring that it receives a good supply of oxygen, and leave the filled container in a warm place. After 1 month, strain out the vinegar. The "mother" can be kept and the process repeated indefinitely as long as fresh alcohol is added to feed the "mother." To make flavored vinegars, immediately after straining, steep the flavoring of your choice in the strained vinegar. Leave for as long as possible before use. Once opened, store in a cool place.

APPETIZERS

Fresh Figs with Edible Flowers

4 ripe figs
½ cup cottage cheese
8 thin slices smoked chicken
Few red and white Belgian
   endive leaves
Few butter lettuce leaves
Few edible flowers

Dressing
¼ cup sunflower oil
3 tablespoons apple with honey
   vinegar
½ teaspoon mustard powder
¼ teaspoon each salt and freshly
   ground black pepper
3 tablespoons Neufchâtel or other
   soft white cheese

*W*ipe the figs, then quarter them without cutting through, open up, and place a mound of cottage cheese in the center of each fig.

Form the smoked chicken slices into rolls. Divide the endive and lettuce leaves among four plates, and arrange the figs and chicken rolls on top. Garnish with edible flowers.

Blend the dressing ingredients and serve alongside. *Serves 4.*

Scallops Ceviche

8 large scallops (fresh or fully
    defrosted), cleaned
Scant ¾ cup lime juice
3 tablespoons sherry vinegar
    or lemongrass vinegar
4–6 cups salad leaves
1 teaspoon grated lime zest

Salsa
3 tablespoons sunflower oil

1 tablespoon tomato paste
1 tablespoon sherry vinegar
1 green Anaheim chile, seeded, and
    finely chopped
3 ripe tomatoes, peeled, seeded,
    and chopped
3 scallions, trimmed and finely
    chopped
Dash liquid hot pepper seasoning
¼ teaspoon salt

Lightly rinse the scallops and place in a glass bowl. Blend the lime juice and vinegar, pour over the scallops, cover, and marinate in the refrigerator for at least 12 hours. Stir occasionally.

For the salsa, blend the oil, tomato paste, and vinegar together. Stir in the chopped chile, tomatoes, and scallions, add the liquid hot pepper seasoning, and salt. Mix lightly, set aside for 1 hour.

Drain the scallops, arrange them on a bed of salad leaves, and garnish with the lime zest. Serve with the salsa. *Serves 4.*

NOTE When planning to eat shellfish raw, purchase only from a reputable market. Be sure shellfish is commercially grown, fresh, and clean.

Clams Marinière

2 pounds clams
1 tablespoon salt
⅔ cup dry white wine
1 onion, sliced
1 small lemon, sliced
½ cup chopped parsley
2 bay leaves
10 peppercorns, lightly bruised
⅔ cup water
3 tablespoons sherry vinegar or Cabernet Sauvignon vinegar
¼ cup half-and-half

*D*iscard any clams that are open or damaged. Scrub the clams thoroughly in plenty of cold water, then place in a large bowl. Cover completely with salted water and allow to stand for 30 minutes. Rinse and let stand again, completely covered in cold water, until needed. Meanwhile, place the wine, onion, lemon, half the parsley and rest of the herbs, peppercorns, and ⅔ cup water in a large saucepan. Bring to a boil over high heat, then reduce heat and simmer gently for 15 minutes.

14

Drain the clams, then add to the court bouillon in the pan. Cover and cook on high heat for 7–10 minutes, or until all the clams have opened. Holding the lid tightly, shake the pan frequently, or stir the clams with a wooden spoon.

Using a slotted spoon, remove the clams to a large serving bowl, discarding any that have not opened; keep warm. Strain the liquid remaining in the pan and return it to the cleaned pan. Bring to a boil and cook vigorously on high heat for 5 minutes, or until reduced by half. Reduce heat, add the vinegar, and cook for 2 minutes more. Remove the pan from the heat, stir in the half-and-half and remaining parsley, pour it over the clams, and serve immediately. *Serves 4.*

Insalata di Funghi

3 tablespoons garlic-flavored olive oil
1–2 cloves garlic, crushed or minced
1–2 green jalapeño chiles, seeded and chopped
*¼ pound each chanterelle, oyster, and button mushrooms,
wiped and thickly sliced*
¼ cup white wine vinegar or Cabernet Sauvignon vinegar
Pinch salt and ½ teaspoon freshly ground black pepper
1 tablespoon minced fresh flat-leaved parsley
Few shavings black truffle, optional
1 tablespoon finely chopped fresh chives
1 teaspoon orange zest, cut into julienne strips

*H*eat the oil, and gently sauté the garlic and chiles over medium heat for 3 minutes. Add the mushrooms, and continue to cook for 3 minutes, or until the mushrooms have softened slightly. Stir in the vinegar, seasoning, and parsley. Serve warm, sprinkled with a few shavings of black truffle, if desired. Garnish with the chives and orange zest. *Serves 4.*

Fresh Pear, Brie & Pecan Medley

4 ripe pears
3 tablespoons lemon juice
About 6 ounces ripe Brie
Few frisée and arugula leaves
½ cup pecan halves
½ cup alpine strawberries

Dressing
¼ cup crème fraîche
1 teaspoon whole grain mustard
⅓ cup extra-virgin olive oil
¼ cup champagne vinegar or
    blush wine vinegar
1 teaspoon green peppercorns

*W*ipe the pears and cut them in half. Discard the core. Slice the pears thinly and brush with lemon juice. Cut the Brie into thin slivers. Arrange the salad leaves and pears on four individual serving plates, with the Brie slices on top. Sprinkle with the pecans and alpine strawberries.

Blend together the crème fraîche and mustard. Gradually stir in the oil, vinegar, and peppercorns. Drizzle over the pears and serve immediately. *Serves 4.*

Chinese Hot & Sour Soup

¼ pound carrots, peeled

2 stalks celery, trimmed

4-inch piece cucumber, peeled and seeded

¼ pound shiitake mushrooms

1 tablespoon olive oil

4¼ cups chicken broth

3 tablespoons rice vinegar

1 tablespoon soy sauce

1 tablespoon dry sherry

1 clove garlic, crushed or minced

1–2 serrano chiles, seeded, if preferred, and finely sliced

2 teaspoons peeled and grated fresh ginger

½ cup snow peas, trimmed

¼ pound bamboo shoots, trimmed and sliced

1 rounded tablespoon cornstarch

¼ cup water

3 tablespoons Chinese black vinegar or balsamic vinegar

3 scallions, trimmed and sliced diagonally

Cut the carrot, celery, and cucumber into julienne strips. Wipe, or lightly rinse, the mushrooms and cut into ¼-inch slices. Heat the oil in a medium skillet over medium-high heat, and lightly sauté the mushrooms for 2 minutes, or until just softened. Drain on paper towels, squeezing out any excess oil, and reserve.

Place the broth, rice vinegar, soy sauce, and sherry in a large pan with the garlic, chiles, and ginger. Bring to a boil over high heat, then reduce to a simmer. Add the carrot and celery, cook for 2 minutes, then add the cucumber, mushrooms, snow peas, and bamboo shoots.

Blend the cornstarch to a smooth paste with ¼ cup of water. Bring the soup to a boil over high heat, then stir in the cornstarch paste. Continue to stir over high heat until the soup thickens, then add the vinegar. Serve piping hot, sprinkled with the scallion garnish. *Serves 4.*

Mussels with Lemongrass

16 mussels, cooked in their shells
2–3 lemongrass stalks, chopped
2 serrano chile peppers, seeded
   and sliced
2 cloves garlic, crushed or minced
1 tablespoon capers, coarsely chopped

3 tablespoons white wine vinegar
   or lemongrass vinegar
¼ cup safflower oil
½ teaspoon honey
Few minced fresh cilantro leaves

Shell the mussels and place in a shallow dish. Wash, dry, and reserve the shells. Place the lemongrass, 1 chile, garlic, capers, vinegar, oil, and honey in a saucepan. Bring to a boil and cook on high heat for 3 minutes. Stir in most of the cilantro. When cool, pour over the mussels, cover, and chill for at least 1 hour.

To serve, drain the mussels and replace in their shells. Strain the marinade and drizzle a little over each mussel. Garnish with the remaining cilantro and chile, and serve. *Serves 4.*

Melon with Parma Ham & Passion Fruit Dressing

1 pale-fleshed melon, peeled and seeded
8 thin slices Parma ham
Few radicchio and sorrel leaves
1 cup cubed feta cheese
Few nasturtium blossoms

Dressing

3 ripe passion fruits
Pinch each mustard powder, salt, and freshly ground black pepper
2 tablespoons champagne vinegar or oregano-flavored white wine vinegar
¼ cup Neufchâtel or other soft white cheese

Cut the melon into 8 small wedges. Roll a strip of ham around each melon wedge. Decorate a serving platter with the salad leaves and arrange the wedges on top. Sprinkle the cheese on top.

Rub the passion fruit through a strainer, then stir in the mustard, seasoning, and vinegar. Blend in the soft cheese. Drizzle a little of the dressing over the melon salad and serve the rest on the side. Garnish with the flower blossoms. *Serves 4.*

MAIN DISH SALADS

Warm Potato Salad

¾ *pound baby red potatoes*

Scant ½ pound baby carrots

2 very small Bermuda or red onions,
thinly sliced

1 cup seedless grapes, halved

1 green eating apple

4–6 cups mixed salad leaves

2 teaspoons finely chopped fresh
chives

Dressing

¼ cup herb vinegar

¼ cup walnut oil

1 teaspoon whole grain mustard

2 teaspoons orange blossom
honey

¼ teaspoon salt and ½ teaspoon
freshly ground black pepper

Scrub the potatoes and carrots. Cook separately in lightly salted boiling water over high heat, until tender. Drain, cut the potatoes in halves or quarters, and the carrots, if large, in half. Place potatoes and carrots in a bowl with the onion and grapes. Core and chop the apple and add to the vegetables. Line a salad bowl with the mixed leaves and fill with the potato mixture.

In a saucepan over medium heat, stir together the vinegar, oil, mustard, honey, and the seasoning. Pour the warm dressing over the potato salad. Garnish with the chives. *Serves 4.*

Smoked Salmon with Raspberries

½ pound fresh asparagus, trimmed
* and sliced diagonally*
1 tablespoon walnut oil
2 ripe avocados
2 tablespoons lemon juice
Mixture of radicchio, frisée,
* and arugula leaves*
½ pound smoked salmon or trout,
* cut into strips*

¼ pound fresh raspberries
Few Pecorino cheese shavings

Dressing
¼ cup raspberry vinegar
3 tablespoons walnut oil
½ teaspoon mustard powder
½ cup sour cream

Sauté the asparagus in oil over medium heat for 5 minutes, stirring frequently; drain and set aside. Peel and dice the avocados, sprinkle with lemon juice, and reserve. Arrange the salad leaves on a platter. Top with the asparagus, avocado, fish, and raspberries.

Blend the vinegar, oil, and mustard until well mixed; stir in the sour cream. Drizzle the dressing over the salad; top with cheese shavings and serve. *Serves 4.*

23

Warm Asparagus & Chanterelle Salad

6 tablespoons virgin olive oil
¾ pound fresh asparagus, trimmed and sliced diagonally
½ pound chanterelle mushrooms, wiped and sliced
1 clove garlic, crushed or minced
½ pound baby spinach, rinsed
3 tablespoons pine nuts, toasted
Scant ½ cup chopped sun-dried tomatoes
3 tablespoons balsamic vinegar or red wine vinegar
½ teaspoon mustard powder
½ teaspoon superfine sugar
¼ teaspoon coarse or kosher salt and ½ teaspoon
freshly ground black pepper
Few shavings black truffle (optional)
1 orange, cut into small wedges

*H*eat 1 tablespoon of the oil in a skillet over medium heat. Sauté the asparagus for 5 minutes; drain and reserve. In the same pan over medium heat, sauté the mushrooms and garlic in 4 tablespoons oil for 2 minutes, or until softened. Add the spinach, and cook for 30 seconds or just until wilted. Return the asparagus to the pan, adding the pine nuts and sun-dried tomatoes. Transfer to a serving dish.

Blend the remaining 2 tablespoons oil with the vinegar, mustard, sugar, and seasoning in a bowl, pour it over the salad, and toss lightly. Sprinkle with shavings of truffle, if using, and garnish with the orange wedges. *Serves 4.*

Salmon Kebabs with Cucumber Salsa

1 pound fresh salmon fillet, skinned and cut into 1½-inch cubes
2 shallots, finely sliced
2 bay leaves
Few parsley sprigs
5 white peppercorns, lightly crushed
⅓ cup tarragon vinegar
3 tablespoons virgin olive oil
2 limes, cut into 8 wedges
Few tarragon sprigs
2 teaspoons grated lime zest

Salsa

½ small cucumber, peeled, seeded, and finely chopped
1 clove garlic, crushed or minced
4 scallions, trimmed and chopped
2 ripe tomatoes, peeled, seeded, drained, and chopped
1 tablespoon tarragon vinegar
1 tablespoon lime juice
¼ teaspoon each salt and freshly ground black pepper

*A*rrange the salmon in a shallow dish. Sprinkle with the sliced shallots, herbs, and peppercorns. Blend the vinegar and oil together, pour the mixture over the salmon, cover, and marinate in the refrigerator for at least 30 minutes to allow the flavors to develop.

Meanwhile, make the salsa. Place the cucumber in a bowl with the garlic, scallions, and tomatoes; add the vinegar, lime juice, and seasoning. Mix well, then cover, and let stand so that the flavors develop.

Drain the salmon and thread alternately with the lime wedges onto skewers. Brush with the remaining marinade and cook under a preheated broiler for 3–4 minutes, turning at least once. Brush again with the marinade to keep the salmon moist and succulent. Garnish with the tarragon and lime zest; serve with the cucumber salsa. *Serves 4.*

Lobster with Champagne Sauce

1 onion, sliced

1 large carrot, peeled and sliced

2 stalks celery, trimmed and chopped

1 bouquet garni

Few parsley sprigs

$^2/_3$ cup champagne or dry white wine

3 tablespoons champagne wine
  vinegar

2 live lobsters

Few mixed salad leaves

2 pink grapefruits, peeled and
  segmented

4-inch piece cucumber, peeled,
  seeded, and cut into 2-inch long
  julienne strips

Caviar

Sauce

2 shallots, peeled and chopped

$1^1/_4$ cups champagne

1 tablespoon unsalted butter

2 tablespoons all-purpose white flour

1 tablespoon champagne wine
  vinegar

Scant $^1/_2$ cup sour cream

Pinch salt and $^1/_2$ teaspoon freshly
ground white pepper

*P*lace the onion, carrot, celery, herbs, champagne or white wine, and vinegar in a large pot. Add 1¼ cups water, bring to a boil, and simmer gently for 10 minutes. Return to a boil, add the lobsters, cover, and cook for about 15 minutes over medium heat, or until the lobsters have turned bright orange. Remove from heat, and allow to rest for 5 minutes. Transfer the lobsters to a platter, and let sit until cool enough to handle. Cut the lobsters in half lengthwise, remove the meat, discarding the inedible parts, and cut into bite-size pieces.

Rinse the shells and line with salad leaves. Mix the lobster meat with the grapefruit and cucumber, and return to the shells.

Place the shallots in a pan with the champagne, and boil until the liquid reduces to about ¾ cup. Strain, and discard the shallots. Blend the butter and flour together to form a paste. Bring the reduced champagne to a boil, then whisk in small spoonfuls of the butter paste. Cook, whisking continually until thickened. Remove from the heat, then stir in the vinegar and sour cream with seasoning. Return to a gentle heat to warm.

Drizzle a little sauce over the lobsters and garnish with caviar just before serving. Serve warm or cold with the remaining sauce. *Serves 4.*

ENTRÉES

Piquant Chicken with Pink Grapefruit

4 chicken breast halves, skinned and boned

3 tablespoons virgin olive oil

¼ cup red wine vinegar or grapefruit vinegar

1 tablespoon soy sauce

2 tablespoons red currant jelly

2 cloves garlic, crushed or minced

2 pink grapefruits, peeled and segmented

Pinch coarse or kosher salt and ½ teaspoon freshly ground black pepper

1 teaspoon cornstarch

3 tablespoons water

4–6 cups salad leaves

Few chervil sprigs

Rinse and wipe the chicken breasts and place them in a shallow dish. In a saucepan over medium heat, combine the olive oil, vinegar, soy sauce, jelly, and garlic, stirring until smooth. Cool slightly, then pour the mixture over the chicken. Cover and marinate in the refrigerator for at least 1 hour.

Heat the oven to 400°F about 15 minutes before cooking. Drain the chicken, reserve the marinade, and place each breast

on a small square of foil. Pour a little marinade over the chicken, then fold the foil into packets. Roast the packets in the oven for 15–20 minutes, or until cooked. Five minutes before the end of cooking time, turn back the foil and distribute the grapefruit segments over the chicken breasts.

Place the reserved marinade in a small saucepan with the seasoning and bring to a boil. Blend the cornstarch to a smooth paste with 3 tablespoons water; add it to the marinade and cook over high heat, stirring, until smooth and thickened. Arrange the salad leaves on a platter. Transfer the chicken and grapefruit to the platter and pour the sauce over. Garnish with the chervil. *Serves 4.*

NOTE This dish also works well with duck breasts.

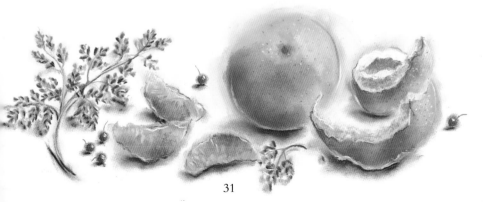

Turkey, Mushroom & Cranberry Stir-fry

⅓ cup sunflower oil

1 pound boneless turkey breast, cubed

1 Bermuda or red onion, peeled and cut into 1-inch dice

2 cloves garlic, crushed or minced

1 cup each chanterelle, oyster, and button mushrooms,
wiped and thickly sliced

½ cup turkey or chicken broth

⅓ cup orange juice

⅓ cup lightly packed soft brown sugar

1½ cups fresh cranberries

2 teaspoons cornstarch

3 tablespoons balsamic vinegar

½ tablespoon chopped fresh cilantro

*H*eat 3 tablespoons of the oil in a wok. Sauté the turkey in batches for 5 minutes, stirring frequently. Drain and reserve. Add 1 tablespoon of the oil to the pan, and sauté the onion and garlic for 2–3 minutes; drain and reserve. Stir in the remaining oil and the mushrooms, and continue cooking for 1 minute. Return the turkey and onions to the wok,

32

along with the broth, orange juice, sugar, and cranberries. Bring to a boil, then cover and simmer for 5 minutes, or until the cranberries just begin to "pop." Meanwhile, blend the cornstarch with the vinegar to form a paste, and add to the wok. Cook for 1 minute, or until thickened. Serve garnished with the cilantro. *Serves 4.*

NOTE This recipe will work well if either chicken or beef fillet is substitued for the turkey. Or vary the type of mushrooms used — try shiitake or any other variety.

Duck Breasts with Kumquats

4 duck breast halves, boned

1 tablespoon sunflower oil

2 cloves garlic, crushed or minced

1–2 serrano chiles, seeded and
  chopped

1 onion, thinly sliced

2 teaspoons whole grain mustard

1/4 teaspoon salt and 1/2 teaspoon
  freshly ground black pepper

1 tablespoon soft brown sugar

1/4 cup apple with honey vinegar

2/3 cup chicken or vegetable broth

About 1/3 pound kumquats, halved

4 scallions, trimmed and sliced
  diagonally

Few cilantro sprigs

*R*inse and wipe the duck breasts and make 3 deep slashes across the skin. Heat the oil in a large skillet and brown the duck on all sides over medium-high heat. Remove from the pan and drain on paper towels. Pour off all but one tablespoon fat, add the garlic, chiles, and onion to the pan, and sauté over medium heat for 3 minutes, or until slightly softened. Stir in the whole grain mustard, seasoning, sugar, vinegar, and broth. Bring to a boil, then reduce the heat. Return the duck to the pan, cover, and simmer over low heat for 15 minutes.

34

Add all but 2 kumquats to the pan and continue simmering for 5 minutes, or until the duck is tender.

Blanch the scallions for 2 minutes in boiling water, then drain. Slice the reserved kumquats. Arrange the duck on a warmed serving platter, pour the sauce over, and garnish with the scallions, cilantro, and remaining 2 kumquats sliced. Serve with freshly cooked pasta and a mixed green salad. *Serves 4.*

NOTE Try substituting fresh pitted cherries, when they are in season, for the kumquats.

Italian Calf Liver

1 pound calf liver
1 onion, sliced
2 bay leaves, coarsely torn
Few parsley sprigs
Few fresh sage leaves
5 peppercorns, lightly crushed
1 tablespoon red currant jelly, warmed
¼ cup walnut oil
¼ cup sherry vinegar or sage berry vinegar
3 tablespoons flour, seasoned with salt and pepper to taste
2 cloves garlic, crushed or minced
1 each red and orange bell peppers, seeded and sliced
Scant ¼ cup sun-dried tomatoes, coarsely chopped
2 teaspoons soy sauce
⅔ cup chicken broth
½ teaspoon freshly ground black pepper
½ tablespoon coarsely chopped fresh sage leaves

Cut the liver into very thin slices and place in a shallow dish. Scatter the onion, bay leaves, parsley, sage, and peppercorns on top. Blend the jelly, 1 tablespoon of the oil, and the vinegar together. Pour the mixture over the liver, cover, and marinate in the refrigerator for 30 minutes, turning at least once.

Remove the liver from the marinade, strain the liquid, and reserve. Coat the liver in the seasoned flour. Add the remaining oil to a skillet over medium heat. Sauté the garlic and bell peppers for 5 minutes, remove with a slotted spoon, and reserve. Add the liver, turn the heat to high, and brown on all sides. Return the garlic and bell peppers to the pan, add the reserved marinade, the sun-dried tomatoes, soy sauce, and broth. Bring to a boil, then reduce heat and simmer for 5 minutes, or until the liver is cooked. Add the pepper and serve garnished with the sage. *Serves 4.*

Lamb with Apricot Relish

4 rib lamb chops
1 teaspoon crushed garlic
1 tablespoon hazelnut oil
3 tablespoons cider vinegar
3 tablespoons apricot nectar or orange juice
3 bay leaves, coarsely torn
Few mint sprigs
1 tablespoon green peppercorns
4 fresh apricots

Relish

3/4 cup pitted dried apricots, finely chopped
2/3 cup apricot nectar or orange juice
3 tablespoons cider vinegar
1 tablespoon dark brown sugar
1 teaspoon ground cinnamon
1/2 teaspoon freshly grated nutmeg
1/2 teaspoon butter

Place the lamb chops in a shallow dish. Combine the garlic, oil, vinegar, fruit juice, bay leaves, half of the mint sprigs, and peppercorns and pour the mixture over the lamb. Cover and marinate in the refrigerator for at least 1 hour.

Preheat the broiler to high. Drain the rib lamb chops, and place on the broiler rack. Brush with a little marinade, then broil each side for 2 minutes. Reduce the heat to medium and continue to broil for 6–8 minutes each side, or until cooked.

Meanwhile, make the relish. Place the dried apricots in a pan with the fruit juice, vinegar, and sugar. Simmer gently over low heat for 10–15 minutes, then blend to a thick consistency. Add the cinnamon, nutmeg, and butter, and stir well. Serve spooned over the lamb chops, and garnish with halved fresh apricots and extra mint sprigs.
Serves 4.

Pork Medallions with Plum Sauce

1 pound boned pork loin, cut into 8 medallions,
each about 1 inch thick
2 cloves garlic, crushed or minced
4½ tablespoons dry white wine
3 tablespoons sweet blackberry vinegar (see page 61)
1 tablespoon safflower oil
Few flat-leaved parsley sprigs

Sauce
¾ pound dark red plums, pitted
3 tablespoons red currant jelly
7 tablespoons water
1 tablespoon hoisin sauce
½–1 teaspoon arrowroot
2 tablespoons balsamic vinegar

*P*lace the pork in a shallow dish and distribute garlic on top. Combine the wine, vinegar, and oil; pour over the pork, cover, and marinate in the refrigerator for at least 30 minutes. Just before cooking, preheat the broiler to high. Drain the pork, place on the broiler rack, and broil for 2 minutes a side. Reduce the heat to medium and continue cooking for 3–4 minutes on each side, or until cooked to your liking.

Wash the plums, and reserve 2 for garnish. Coarsely chop the remaining plums. Place them in a saucepan with the jelly and 4 tablespoons of water. Bring to a boil, then reduce the heat to low and simmer for 10 minutes, or until the plums are cooked. Strain, discard the plums, return the liquid to the pan, add the hoisin sauce, and bring back to a boil. Blend the arrowroot with 3 tablespoons water, stir into the sauce, and cook over high heat until it is clear and thickened. Turn down the heat, add the balsamic vinegar, stir until well blended, and transfer to a sauceboat.

Garnish the pork with slices of reserved plum and parsley sprigs, and accompany with the sauce. *Serves 4.*

Seafood Brochettes

1 pound fresh seafood of one variety,
    such as monkfish, salmon, tuna,
    or large shrimp
Few dill sprigs
2 cloves garlic, crushed or minced
6 tablespoons champagne vinegar
¼ cup virgin olive oil

Zest and juice of ½ lemon
Pinch salt and ½ teaspoon freshly
    ground black pepper
¼ cup sesame seeds
Few bay leaves
4 lemon and lime wedges

*D*iscard the bones and skin from the fish and cut into cubes. If using shrimp, remove the shrimp shell — except for the tail — and remove the fine legs and dark intestinal membrane. Place the seafood in a shallow dish and sprinkle with half the dill and the garlic. Blend the vinegar, oil, lemon zest and juice, and seasoning. Pour over the fish mixture, cover, and chill for at least 30 minutes.

Preheat broiler to high. Drain the seafood, roll in sesame seeds, and thread onto skewers, interspersed with bay leaves. Brush the brochettes with marinade and broil, turning frequently and brushing with more marinade, for 5 minutes or until just cooked. Garnish with the remaining dill and lemon and lime wedges. *Serves 4.*

Chicken Breasts with Pink Peppercorns

4 chicken breast halves, skinned
    and boned
1 tablespoon sunflower oil
3 tablespoons raspberry vinegar
1 tablespoon acacia honey

Grated zest and juice of 1 large orange
Few mint sprigs, bruised
3 tablespoons pink peppercorns
Few mint sprigs
Few fresh raspberries

*R*inse and dry the chicken breasts. Heat the oil in a skillet over high heat and seal the meat. Remove from the heat, lift out the breasts, and wipe the pan clean. Return the chicken to the skillet. Mix the vinegar, honey, grated orange zest and juice, and drizzle the mixture over the chicken. Add some of the mint and the peppercorns to the skillet, and bring to a boil. Reduce the heat to low, cover, and simmer gently for 15–20 minutes, turning once or twice, until the chicken is cooked. Discard the mint, arrange the chicken on a warmed platter, and pour the pan juices on top. Garnish with the remaining mint and some raspberries. *Serves 4.*

Beef Fillet in Spicy Vinegar Sauce

4 thick slices of beef fillet (about ¾ pound), trimmed
2 cloves garlic, crushed or minced
1 tablespoon chopped mixed herbs, such as thyme,
oregano, sage, and parsley
¼ teaspoon salt and ½ teaspoon freshly ground black pepper
⅓ cup red wine vinegar
2 teaspoons honey
⅔ cup red wine
1 tablespoon tomato paste
1 teaspoon arrowroot
1 tablespoon water
1 teaspoon brown sugar
½ tablespoon minced flat-leaved parsley
1 leaf frisée, shredded

Place the beef fillets in a shallow dish. In a bowl, mix the garlic, herbs, seasoning, vinegar, honey, red wine, and tomato paste. Stir well to blend, pour on top of the beef, and cover. Marinate for 1 hour in the refrigerator.

Preheat the broiler to high. Place the meat on the

broiler rack and broil about 2 minutes on each side to brown. Turn down the broiler to medium and continue to cook for 3 minutes on each side, or until done to your liking.

Strain the marinade, bring to a boil, and cook on high for 5 minutes, or until reduced by half. Blend the arrowroot with the water, stir into the saucepan with the sugar, and cook until thickened. Pour it over the fillets and sprinkle with the parsley and frisée. *Serves 4.*

Turkey Brochettes with Apple & Orange Salsa

¾ pound boneless, skinless turkey breast

Pinch salt and ½ teaspoon freshly ground black pepper

¼ cup sunflower oil

¼ cup cider with honey vinegar or apple with honey vinegar

2 teaspoons soy sauce

2 teaspoons wildflower or orange blossom honey, warmed

½ cup apple or orange juice

1 medium onion, sliced

2 cloves garlic, crushed or minced

1 medium orange, cut into wedges

1 medium red apple, cored and cut into wedges

Few mint sprigs

Salsa

1 small green apple, cored

1 large orange, peeled and segmented

1 small Bermuda or red onion, peeled

1 tablespoon apple with honey vinegar

1 tablespoon finely chopped fresh mint

Pinch salt and ¼ teaspoon freshly ground black pepper

Rinse the turkey, and pat dry with paper towels. Cut into 1½-inch cubes, and then place in a shallow dish. Season with the salt and pepper. Mix together the oil, vinegar, soy sauce, honey, and juice, then pour the mixture over the turkey. Sprinkle with the onion and garlic, cover, and marinate in the refrigerator for at least 1 hour, stirring occasionally.

To make the salsa, finely chop the green apple, orange, and onion; mix well, then drain and place in a bowl. Mix in the remaining ingredients. Cover and chill for 30 minutes to allow the flavors to develop.

Drain the turkey, then thread onto skewers alternately with the red apple and orange wedges. Brush with the marinade. Broil for 8–10 minutes, or until cooked, turning at least once and brushing occasionally with the marinade. Garnish with mint sprigs and serve with the salsa.
Serves 4.

Pot-roasted Chicken with Grapes

1 free-range chicken (about 3 pounds)
Few thyme, sage, oregano, and rosemary sprigs,
tied in a bunch
1 medium onion, quartered
2 carrots, peeled and thickly sliced
1 fennel bulb, trimmed and cut into thick wedges
½ teaspoon each salt and freshly ground black pepper
¼ cup white wine vinegar or oregano-flavored white wine vinegar
1¼ cups chicken broth or white wine
2 tablespoons butter or margarine, softened
¼ cup all-purpose flour
¼ pound seedless grapes, skinned, if preferred, and halved
¼ cup cream
Few oregano or chervil sprigs

Preheat the oven to 375°F. Rinse and dry the chicken, and place the bundle of herbs inside it. Arrange the prepared vegetables in the bottom of a chicken brick or ovenproof casserole. Season the chicken with half the salt and pepper, and place the chicken on top. Blend the vinegar with the broth and pour it over. Cover the casserole and cook for 1½ hours, or until thoroughly cooked. Transfer the chicken and vegetables to a platter, and keep warm.

Strain the pan juices into a saucepan and add enough water to make up to 2½ cups. Bring to a boil over high heat. Beat the butter and flour together to make a paste. Drip small spoonfuls of it into the pan juices, beating vigorously. Cook for 2 minutes, or until the sauce is smooth and glossy. Reduce the heat to low, add three-quarters of the grapes, and simmer for 2 minutes. Adjust the seasoning, remove the pan from the heat, and stir in the cream. Serve the chicken garnished with the remaining grapes and the fresh herbs, and accompanied by the sauce. *Serves 4.*

NOTE Substitute two Rock Cornish game hens for the chicken and shorten the cooking time by about 30 minutes.

Warm Monkfish & Persimmon

1 pound monkfish, skinned and cleaned

3 cloves garlic, peeled and slivered

Few each dill and thyme sprigs

3 tablespoons olive oil

3 tablespoons sweet blackberry vinegar (see page 61) or blueberry vinegar

2 ripe persimmons

Mixed salad greens and herb leaves

Few tarragon sprigs

Dressing

1 teaspoon whole grain mustard

4 tablespoons extra-virgin olive oil

3 tablespoons sweet blackberry vinegar or blueberry vinegar

1 teaspoon sugar

Pinch salt and ½ teaspoon freshly ground black pepper

*R*inse and dry the fish, make small incisions, and insert the garlic. Arrange the fish in a dish, and scatter the herbs over. Blend the oil and vinegar, pour the mixture over the fish, cover, and marinate for at least 1 hour, turning frequently.

Preheat the oven to 425°F. Using a slotted spoon, remove the fish and place on a large sheet of foil. Strain the marinade and pour it over. Fold the foil over to make a packet encasing the

fish. Put in a roasting pan, and bake, for 15–20 minutes, or until cooked. Meanwhile, slice the persimmons and arrange with the greens on a serving platter. Blend the mustard, oil, and vinegar; add the sugar and seasoning. Remove the monkfish and cut it into diagonal slices, discarding the central bone, if any, and arrange on the bed of greens and persimmon. Drizzle with a little dressing; serve the remainder separately. Garnish the monkfish with the tarragon. *Serves 4.*

Sole with Orange & Lettuce

1 pound sole fillets, skinned

3 tablespoons flour, seasoned with pinch each salt and pepper

3 tablespoons sunflower oil

3 tablespoons pine nuts

2 large oranges, peeled and segmented

3 tablespoons orange vinegar or oregano-flavored wine vinegar

2 teaspoons orange blossom honey, warmed

1 large Romaine or other crisp lettuce, shredded

½ tablespoon grated orange zest

Cut the sole into thin strips, about 3 inches in length, and coat in the seasoned flour. Pour 1½ tablespoons of the oil into a skillet, then gently sauté half the sole over medium heat for 1 minute; remove and drain. Repeat with the remaining oil and sole. Add the pine nuts to the oil remaining in the pan, and cook for 1 minute, or until golden. Add the sole, orange segments, vinegar, and honey, and heat gently, stirring for 1 minute. Add the lettuce and heat for 30 seconds. Serve garnished with orange zest. *Serves 4.*

PRESERVES & SAUCES

Sweet & Sour Apricots

1 pound fresh firm apricots, halved and pitted
Scant 1²/₃ cups dark brown sugar
2½ cups white wine vinegar
¼ cup lemon juice
Few strips lemon zest
2 sticks cinnamon, lightly bruised

Cover the apricots with boiling water, let sit for a few seconds, then skin and set aside.

Put the sugar in a wide, shallow pan with the vinegar, lemon juice, zest, and cinnamon. Dissolve over low heat, stirring occasionally. Add the apricots and continue to simmer gently for 10 minutes, or until the fruit is tender but still maintains its shape. Using a slotted spoon, lift the fruit from the syrup and pack into 2 sterilized 1-pound jars. Turn the heat to high and boil the remaining syrup until reduced by half. Pour the syrup over the apricots, seal, and label. Let mature for at least 3 weeks. Use within 6 months. *Makes about 2 pounds.*

Sweet & Hot Vegetable Pickle

1 each red and green bell peppers,
  seeded and thickly sliced
4 medium carrots, cut in 1–1½
  inch slices
1 medium cauliflower, in small
  flowerets
3 pounds baby onions, peeled

1 whole head garlic, cloves peeled
  but whole
1 cup salt
1 quart malt vinegar
¾ cup water
1–1½ cups sugar
1 teaspoon pickling spice

*I*n a glass bowl, alternate layers of vegetables and salt, finishing with a layer of salt. Cover and let stand until the next day. Drain, then rinse to remove the salt. Dry thoroughly.

In a stainless steel saucepan, bring the vinegar, water, sugar, and pickling spice just to a boil, stirring constantly.

Meanwhile, divide the vegetables between 6 warm, sterilized jars. Pour the hot vinegar mixture over the vegetables, making sure they are completely covered. Seal and let stand in a cool dark place for at least 2 weeks. Use within 2 months. *Makes about 6 pounds.*

Green Tomato & Cilantro Relish

3 pounds green tomatoes, washed and chopped

1 large cucumber, peeled and chopped

2 tablespoons salt

3 cloves garlic, chopped

1 red bell pepper, seeded and chopped

3 cups white wine vinegar

½ cup brown sugar

1 tablespoon whole grain mustard

1 tablespoon coriander seeds

3 tablespoons chopped cilantro

Put the tomatoes and cucumber in a bowl, sprinkle with salt, cover, and leave overnight. Drain and rinse the vegetables thoroughly. Put them into a large pan with the garlic and red pepper. Blend the vinegar with the sugar, mustard, and coriander seeds, and add to the pan. Stir gently over low heat, until the sugar has dissolved. Raise the heat to boiling, then reduce and simmer for 50 minutes, or until the vegetables are soft. Stir in the chopped cilantro. Cool slightly before packing into 4 warm, sterilized 1-pound jars. Seal and label. Let mature for about 1 month. Use within 6 months. *Makes about 4 pounds.*

Spiced Pears

2 pounds firm pears, peeled, cored, and quartered
Juice of 1 lemon
1¼ cups green peppercorn vinegar or cider vinegar
1¾ cups light brown sugar
Few strips lemon zest
12 cloves
2 cinnamon sticks, bruised

Put the pears in a large saucepan with the lemon juice and cover them with water. Bring to a boil over high heat, then reduce to low and simmer for 15–20 minutes, or until cooked but still slightly firm. Drain and reserve the pears.

Combine the vinegar, sugar, lemon zest, cloves, cinnamon, and 1¼ cups water in the same saucepan, stirring over low heat until the sugar has dissolved. Increase the heat to high and boil for 10 minutes, or until you have a light syrup. Reduce the heat to low, add the pears, and continue to cook for 10 minutes. Remove the pears, strain the syrup, and allow both to cool. Pack the pears into 2 sterilized 1-pound preserving jars, cover with the strained syrup, seal, and label. Use within 6 months. *Makes about 2 pounds.*

Rhubarb & Kumquat Chutney

2½ pounds rhubarb

Juice and zest of 1 large orange

3 large onions, chopped

2½ cups malt vinegar

1¼ cups orange vinegar

1½ pounds light brown sugar

1⅓ cups raisins

1 tablespoon mustard seeds

1 tablespoon mixed peppercorns

1 teaspoon allspice

¾ pound kumquats, seeded and
  coarsely chopped

*T*rim the rhubarb into small lengths. Put the orange juice and zest, and the rhubarb, into a deep, shallow pan with the onions, vinegars, sugar, and raisins. Simmer gently, stirring occasionally, until the sugar has dissolved. Tie the spices in a square of cheesecloth, and add to the pan with the kumquats. Continue simmering until thick. Discard the spices and pack the chutney into 8 warm, sterilized 1-pound jars. When cool, seal, label, and let mature for 2 weeks. Use within 6 months. *Makes about 8 pounds.*

Mango Chutney

²/₃ cup raisins

²/₃ cup fresh dates, pitted and chopped

1 red bell pepper, seeded and sliced

2–4 serrano chiles, chopped

Scant 2 cups cider vinegar

12 mangoes, peeled, pitted, and sliced

1 pound light brown sugar

2 teaspoons crushed garlic

3 tablespoons peeled and grated
  fresh ginger

1 onion, finely chopped

1 tablespoon salt

¹/₃ cup lemon juice

Put the raisins, dates, red bell pepper, and chiles in a bowl. Pour in half the vinegar, cover, and let stand for 24 hours.

Pour into a wide, shallow pan and add the remaining ingredients. Stir over low heat until the sugar has dissolved. Bring to a boil, reduce the heat to low, and simmer for 1 hour, or until thick. Cool slightly, then put in 3 warm, sterilized 1-pound jars. When cold, seal and label. Let mature for about 1 month. Use within 6 months. *Makes 3 pounds*.

FLAVORED VINEGARS

Have fun combining different flavors. When sealing, either use a nonmetallic lid or place a sheet of plastic wrap over the top of a clean jar or bottle to separate the vinegar from the metal. Vinegar keeps indefinitely, but solids in the jar will discolor and eventually break down.

Nasturtium Vinegar

½ pound freshly picked nasturtium flowers
4 cloves
14 mixed peppercorns
1 teaspoon coriander seeds
1 teaspoon mustard seeds
2 cloves garlic, minced or slivered
1 large onion, finely chopped
2½ pints light malt vinegar or white wine vinegar

Pick through the flowers to remove any dead or damaged material, then rinse lightly, and let dry. Lightly bruise the spices to release their aroma. Divide the ingredients between four 1½-cup bottles or jars, and cover with the vinegar. Seal, and leave undisturbed for 2 months. *Makes 2½ pints.*

Rose Vinegar
1 cup rose petals, preferably scented
3¾ cups wine vinegar

*R*inse and dry the petals. Pack into 3 small (10 fluid ounce) jars, and fill with vinegar. Seal, and leave in the sun for about 1 month, or as long as possible. Strain before using in salad dressings. *Makes scant 5 cups.*

NOTE This is also ideal as a cordial. Stir about 2 tablespoons vinegar into 1 cup water, sweetened with honey. For variety, make with wild violet blossoms and primroses.

Sweet Blackberry Vinegar

2 pounds blackberries, picked over and rinsed
2½ cups white wine vinegar
About 1 pound sugar

Put 1 pound of the blackberries in a large bowl. Add the vinegar and let stand for 24 hours. Strain the berries, reserving the liquid and blackberries separately. Pour the steeped vinegar over the second pound of blackberries and repeat. Return both amounts of reserved blackberries, and leave for another 24 hours. Strain the liquid through cheesecloth into a large saucepan and discard the berries. Add 1 pound sugar to the saucepan for every 2½ cups of juice. Boil over high heat for 30 minutes, remove and cool, then bottle. Keep for 2 months before using. *Makes about 3¾ cups.*

NOTE Adapted from *Summer Drinks and Winter Cordials*, Mrs. C. F. Leyel, 1925.

Rosemary Vinegar

1 pound rosemary sprigs, woody stems discarded
2½ cups cider vinegar

*R*inse and dry half the rosemary, bruising lightly. Place the rosemary in a glass jar, add the vinegar, and cover with a cloth. Let sit for 2 days. Stir with a wooden spoon, then replace the cover. Let sit for 7 days more. Strain the vinegar, and discard the rosemary.

Using the strained vinegar, repeat with the second bunch of rosemary, allowing it to sit for at least 1 month. Pour through a fine strainer, bottle with fresh rosemary sprigs, seal, and store in a cool, dark place. *Makes 2½ cups.*

NOTE This method also works for other herbs, such as mint, dill, thyme, and basil.

Black Currant Vinegar

1 pound black currants
2½ cups malt vinegar
About 1½ pounds sugar

*D*iscard stems and any leaves from the black currants and rinse well. Drain thoroughly, then place in a large bowl. Mash the fruit lightly with a fork or the back of a wooden spoon, pour over the vinegar, cover with a clean cloth, and let stand in a cool place for 3–4 days, stirring occasionally.

Strain the liquid through double thickness of cheesecloth and measure into a wide, shallow pan. For each 2½ cups of liquid extracted, add 1 pound of sugar. Place the pan over low heat and cook gently, stirring occasionally, until the sugar has dissolved. Bring to a boil and cook over high heat for 10 minutes. Cool, then strain into bottles and seal.

Keep in a cool place for up to 6 months. Once opened, use within 2–3 weeks. *Makes 2 pints.*

Index